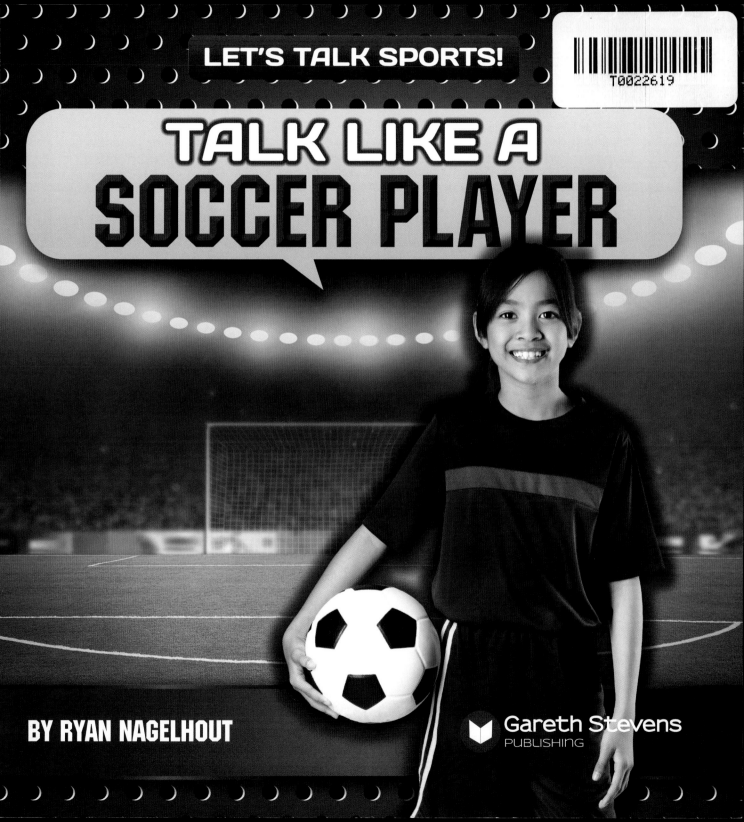

LET'S TALK SPORTS!

T0022619

# TALK LIKE A
# SOCCER PLAYER

BY RYAN NAGELHOUT

Gareth Stevens
PUBLISHING

**Please visit our website, www.garethstevens.com. For a free color catalog of all our high-quality books, call toll free 1-800-542-2595 or fax 1-877-542-2596.**

**Cataloging-in-Publication Data**
Names: Nagelhout, Ryan.
Title: Talk like a soccer player / Ryan Nagelhout.
Description: New York : Gareth Stevens Publishing, 2017. | Series: Let's talk sports! | Includes index.
Identifiers: ISBN 9781482457124 (pbk.) | ISBN 9781482457148 (library bound) | ISBN 9781482457131 (6 pack)
Subjects: LCSH: Soccer–Juvenile literature.
Classification: LCC GV943.25 N33 2017 | DDC 796.334–dc23

First Edition

Published in 2017 by
**Gareth Stevens Publishing**
111 East 14th Street, Suite 349
New York, NY 10003

Copyright © 2017 Gareth Stevens Publishing

Designer: Samantha DeMartin
Editor: Ryan Nagelhout

Photo credits: Title art chudo-yudo/Shutterstock.com; series background Supphachai Salaeman/Shutterstock.com; cover, p. 1 inset Krivosheev Vitaly/Shutterstock.com; cover, p. 1 soccer player Patrick Foto/Shutterstock.com; soccer caption irin-k/Shutterstock.com; p. 4 In Green/Shutterstock.com; p. 5 Bob Thomas/Bob Thomas Sports Photography/Getty Images; pp. 6, 8 EsraKeskinSenay/Shutterstock.com; p. 7 (background) Just2shutter/Shutterstock.com; p. 9 Pressmaster/Shutterstock.com; p. 10 Andrey_Kuzmin/Shutterstock.com; p. 11 Paolo Bona/Shutterstock.com; p. 12 george studio/Shutterstock.com; p. 13 Jamie Squire/Getty Images Sport/Getty Images; pp. 14, 20 Mike Hewitt/Getty Images Sport/Getty Images; pp. 15, 16 Mitch Gunn/Shutterstock.com; p. 17 Boston Globe/Boston Globe/Getty Images; p. 19 Laurence Griffiths/Getty Images Sport/Getty Images; p. 21 Foodpics/Shutterstock.com; p. 22 Christian Petersen/Getty Images Sport/Getty Images; p. 23 Visionhaus/Corbis Sport/Getty Images; p. 25 (scoreboard) tovovan/Shutterstock.com; p. 25 (background) Angela Waye/Shutterstock.com; p. 26 Iurii Osadchi/Shutterstock.com; p. 27 Laszlo Szirtesi/Shutterstock.com; p. 29 Image Source/Getty Images.

Printed in the United States of America

CPSIA compliance information: Batch #CW17GS : For further information contact Gareth Stevens, New York, New York at 1-800-542-2595.

# CONTENTS

Words in the glossary appear in **bold** type
the first time they are used in the text.

# THE BEAUTIFUL GAME

First things first: Is it soccer or football? It's both! Both words are used to describe a game millions of people around the world play. In America, it's called "soccer" because the word "football" is used for American football.

## LEARN THE LINGO

The word "soccer" came from England, where the game was often called "association football." At some point, "association" was shortened to "soc" and later became the word "soccer."

# AROUND THE WORLD

In Spanish-speaking countries, soccer is called *fútbol*. And the famous Brazilian Pelé is **associated** with another term for it—o *jogo bonito*, or "the beautiful game." Now that you know what to call it, let's learn how to talk about this global game.

PELÉ

PELÉ IS ONE OF THE MOST FAMOUS SOCCER PLAYERS IN THE WORLD. HE TRULY PLAYED BEAUTIFUL SOCCER, WHICH MADE MILLIONS WANT TO PLAY THE GAME THEMSELVES.

# TAKE THE PITCH

Soccer is played on a large field, often called a pitch. The name comes from England, where a pitch is a large area of grass used for a certain sport.

SOMETIMES SOCCER IS PLAYED ON **ARTIFICIAL** GRASS. THIS SURFACE, SOMETIMES CALLED "TURF," IS MADE UP OF BLADES OF GRASS MADE FROM PLASTIC.

# SIZING IT UP

Not every field is the same size, but most pitches are from 100 to 130 yards (90 to 120 m) long and 50 to 100 yards (45 to 90 m) wide. **International** matches, or games, are played on pitches from 110 to 120 yards (100 to 110 m) long and 70 to 80 yards (64 to 75 m) wide.

# LINE IT UP

No matter what its size, a soccer pitch looks like a large rectangle. The shorter lines where the front posts of each goal sit are called the goal lines. The longer sidelines on a soccer pitch are called touchlines.

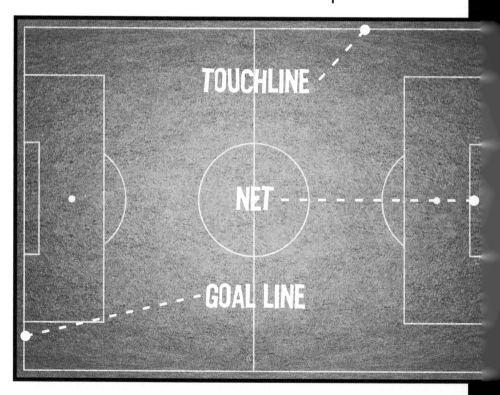

TOUCHLINE

NET

GOAL LINE

# BIG NETS

A large net sits at each end of a soccer pitch. These nets are called goals. The point of soccer is to get a ball into the other team's net. Each team **defends** its net from the other team's attack.

WHEN A PLAYER SCORES, IT'S ALSO CALLED A GOAL. THIS MAY SOUND A BIT CONFUSING, BUT IN SOCCER YOU WANT TO SCORE GOALS BY PUTTING A BALL INTO THE GOAL!

## LEARN THE LINGO

Anything outside the goal lines and touchlines isn't in play. This is also called "out of bounds."

9

A soccer pitch is cut in half by a line. At the middle of the pitch is a point called the center mark. This mark is surrounded by a circle that's 10 yards (9.15 m) across. The ball is put on this mark to start each game.

THE BALL IS PUT ON THE CENTER MARK AFTER A GOAL IS SCORED, TOO. THE TEAM THAT WAS SCORED ON GETS TO START WITH THE BALL ON THAT SPOT.

# IN THE BOX

The **penalty** area is a large box marked off in front of each net. This is sometimes called the "18-yard box" because it extends 18 yards (16.5 m) away from the net. It's sometimes just called the "box."

CLAUDIO MARCHISIO TAKES A CORNER KICK.

11

# FIELDING A TEAM

Each team has 11 people on the pitch in soccer. One player, called a netminder or keeper, stays near the net and tries to keep the other team from scoring. There are three other basic positions in soccer.

4-4-2 FORMATION    4-3-3 FORMATION    4-5-1 FORMATION

**THESE ARE SOME EXAMPLES OF DIFFERENT FORMATIONS IN SOCCER.**

# ALL OVER THE PITCH

Forwards mostly play on the other team's side of the pitch and try to score goals. Midfielders play the middle of the field, which means they play **offense** and defense. Defenders, meanwhile, mostly play in front of their own net.

FORWARD ALEX MORGAN

## LEARN THE LINGO

A team can put its players in many different areas on the pitch. These are called formations and are often talked about using the different numbers of each position on the field.

13

# NO HANDS ON

One reason some people call the game "football" is because most players only use their feet. Only the keeper on each team can use their hands. They can only use their hands inside their own penalty area, though.

KEEPER TIM HOWARD

14

KEEPERS WEAR BIG GLOVES AND OFTEN A DIFFERENT COLOR UNIFORM THAN THEIR TEAMMATES TO HELP THEM STAND OUT. THAT'S HOW YOU KNOW WHICH PLAYER CAN TOUCH THE BALL WITH THEIR HANDS, TOO!

# NOT JUST FEET

All players can use their heads to touch the ball, too. They can also use their knees and chest. They just have to be careful not to use their hands. Otherwise, a "handball" will be called.

PER MERTESACKER HEADS THE BALL.

## LEARN THE LINGO

A handball isn't just called when the ball touches someone's hand. The elbow, wrist, and even the shoulder aren't allowed to touch the ball in soccer.

15

# DRIBBLING DOWN

Because most players can only use their feet, they have great control of the ball with their feet. Running down the field while kicking a soccer ball is called dribbling. The best soccer players can dribble the ball and stay away from defenders without losing control.

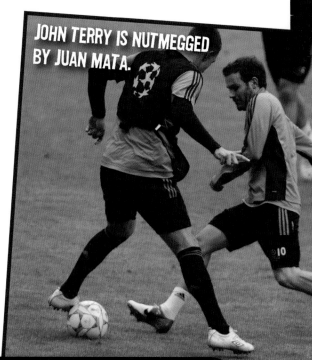

JOHN TERRY IS NUTMEGGED BY JUAN MATA.

## LEARN THE LINGO

Dribbling the ball between a defender's legs is called a "nutmeg." The move only counts if the dribbling player keeps control of the ball after the move!

TEAL BUNBURY CHEST TRAPS THE BALL.

# OTHER WAYS TO CONTROL

Using your head to move the ball is called a "header." Using your chest to settle a ball down and move it to your feet is called a "chest trap."

# PASS IT HERE

Passing is key in soccer. Players need to use their teammates to move the ball long **stretches** down the field. There are many different kinds of passes in soccer.

## THE CROSS

A "cross" is a long pass coming from a player near a touchline. Crossing the ball puts it across and into the middle of the field. Crosses usually put the ball into the box. Players are often waiting there to head or kick the ball on frame, or into the net.

18

CHRIS SMALLING HEADS THE BALL.

## LEARN THE LINGO

A "through ball" is a pass that lets a teammate run past defenders.

DEFENDERS OFTEN TRY TO HEAD BALLS AWAY FROM THE NET
SO THE OTHER TEAM'S PLAYERS DON'T GET SHOTS ON GOAL.

19

# STAYING ONSIDE

You have to stay "onside" when you're trying to score a goal. That means you can only run behind the defense when you have the ball. Otherwise, an official blows a whistle, and the ball is given to the other team.

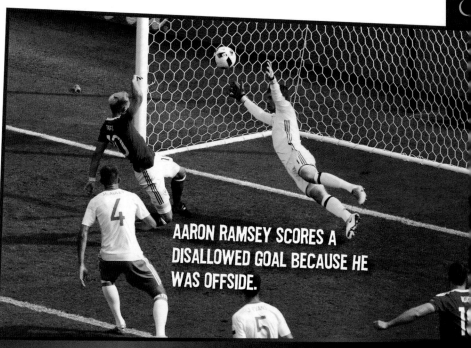

AARON RAMSEY SCORES A DISALLOWED GOAL BECAUSE HE WAS OFFSIDE.

WHEN A TEAM IS OFFSIDE, THE ASSISTANT REFEREE RAISES THE FLAG AND BLOWS A WHISTLE.

# LEARN THE LINGO

One official with a flag watches for offside calls on each side of the field. This official is called the assistant referee.

# TRAP THEM

Defenders often try to "trap" the other team's forwards by moving toward the middle of the field to put them offside. They often spread out along the field in a line, which is why defenders are sometimes called the "back line."

# LEARN THE LINGO

A player who gets behind the defense is on a breakaway, or "on the break."

**SYDNEY LEROUX RUNS PAST A DEFENDER.**

Teams have to beat the offside trap with passing. All players need to be onside when a player from their team is dribbling or has control of the ball. If they pass the ball beyond the defense, though, the player's teammates are "**released**" and can go chase the ball down.

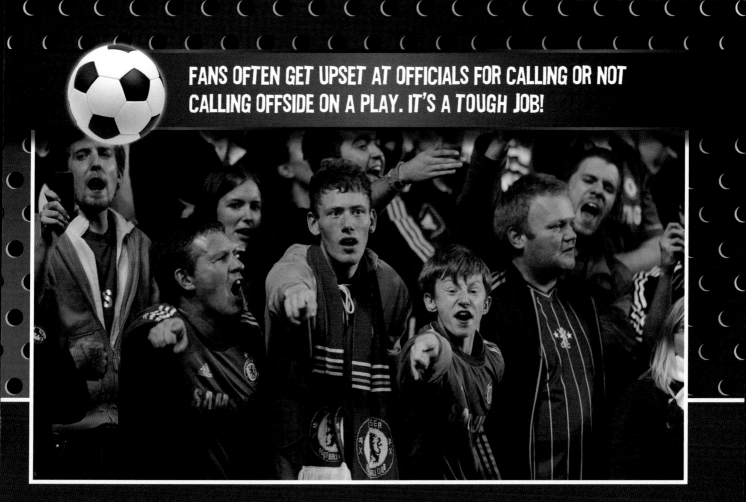

FANS OFTEN GET UPSET AT OFFICIALS FOR CALLING OR NOT CALLING OFFSIDE ON A PLAY. IT'S A TOUGH JOB!

# ALL ALONE

A player that beats the trap by accepting a pass is said to have gotten "behind" the defense. There's a lot of net to shoot at with just the keeper left on defense!

# KEEPING TIME

In professional soccer, the clock never stops. These matches have two halves that last 45 minutes each. A break between each half is called halftime.

## STOPPAGE TIME

Officials keep track of the time lost when the ball goes out of bounds or a player gets hurt. At the end of each half, they add more time onto the game. This is called stoppage time, or penalty time. Stoppage time is added after the 45th and 90th minute, but it's not always kept on a scoreboard.

# LEARN THE LINGO

If a goal is scored 4 minutes and 30 seconds into a match, it's said it was scored in the 5th minute of the match. If it's scored 2 minutes into stoppage time after 90 minutes, it's said to be scored in the 92, or 90+2, on the scoreboard!

HOME   PERIOD   VISITORS

UNLIKE MANY OTHER SPORTS, THE CLOCK COUNTS UP IN SOCCER, NOT DOWN.

# FOULS AND PENALTIES

Fouls are things you can't do in soccer. An official blows a whistle and gives a free kick to the other team.

**26**

BEING **ROUGH** WITH OTHER PLAYERS, SAYING SOMETHING WRONG, OR EVEN HANDBALLS CAN RESULT IN CARDS. YOU NEED TO PLAY SAFE ON THE PITCH!

# RED AND YELLOW

More serious fouls result in cards. These are called "bookings."

A yellow card is a warning card. A red card means a player has

to leave the game. Two yellow cards in a game equal a red card.

Teams that lose players to red cards have to play with one less

person on the pitch!

## LEARN THE LINGO

Fouls in the box result in a penalty kick. That's a free shot
on the goal from the penalty spot in the box!

# MORE ABOUT THE GAME

There are so many more special words used to talk about soccer! A forward is sometimes called a striker. When players score two goals, it's called a brace. Players sitting on the bench are subs, or can be **substituted** into the game.

Coaches in soccer are sometimes called managers. Some games can end in a draw, or a tie. Others go to penalty kicks, where each team gets five chances to score on a keeper from the penalty spot. Keep watching and playing soccer to learn more about the beautiful game!

## LEARN THE LINGO

A keeper who doesn't allow a goal is said to have kept a "clean sheet." It's like a shutout in hockey!

DO YOU HAVE WHAT IT TAKES TO SCORE THE GAME-WINNING GOAL IN A PENALTY SHOOTOUT?

29

# GLOSSARY

**arc:** a curved path that connects two points

**artificial:** made by people and not by nature

**associate:** to connect in thought

**defend:** to keep something safe

**international:** involving two or more countries

**offense:** the team trying to score

**penalty:** having to do with the breaking of rules

**release:** to set free

**rough:** too forceful

**stretch:** a long length of space or distance

**substitute:** to put one person in place of another

# FOR MORE INFORMATION

## BOOKS

Derr, Aaron. *Soccer: An Introduction to Being a Good Sport*. Egremont, MA: Red Chair Press, 2017.

Latham, Andrew. *Soccer Smarts for Kids: 60 Skills, Strategies & Secrets*. Berkeley, CA: Rockridge Press, 2016.

Peterson, Megan Cooley. *Wacky Soccer Trivia: Fun Facts for Every Fan*. North Mankato, MN: Capstone Press, 2017.

## WEBSITES

**Soccer Terms**
*ussoccerplayers.com/soccer-terms*
Learn more about soccer terms on this site.

**Sports: Soccer**
*ducksters.com/sports/soccer.php*
Learn more about soccer here.

# INDEX